Ghostly Graveyards

by Judy Allen

Consultant: Paul F. Johnston, PhD
Historian
Washington, DC

BEARPORT
PUBLISHING

New York, New York

Credits

Cover and title page, © Gino Santa Maria/Shutterstock, © Studio 37/Shutterstock, and © Michael Vorobiev/Shutterstock; 4–5, Kim Jones, © Jakgree/Fotolia, and © Christopher Elwell/Shutterstock; 6, © ESPECIAL/NOTIMEX/Newscom; 7, © Enrique de la Cruz/supernoramx/Flickr; 8, © Alberto Loyo/Shutterstock; 9L, Walkerma/Wikipedia; 9R, © David Ryan/Alamy Stock Photo; 10, © Bertl123/Shutterstock; 11L, © Mikadun/Shutterstock; 11R, © Kim Traynor/Wikipedia; 12, © Rick Drew; 13, © smereka/Shutterstock; 14, © Prioryman/Wikimedia; 15, Wikimedia Commons; 16, © Supannee Hickman/Shutterstock; 17, © Anna Day; 18, © Michael Kleen; 19, © IgorGolovniov/Shutterstock; 20, © Rodel Manabat; 21, © Rocketrod1960/Wikimedia; 22, © Andrew Lake, Greenville Paranormal Research; 23T, © Lario Tus/Dreamstime; 23B, © Zacarias Pereira Da Mata/Dreamstime; 24, © Adwo/Shutterstock; 25, © Robert Wright; 26, © D. Trozzo/Alamy; 27L, © Carmen Rieb/Shutterstock; 27R, © Remisser/English Wikipedia; 31, © Eugenio Marongiu/Shutterstock; 32, © Hitdelight/Shutterstock.

Publisher: Kenn Goin
Senior Editor: Joyce Tavolacci
Creative Director: Spencer Brinker
Design: Dawn Beard Creative
Cover: Kim Jones
Photo Researcher: Picture Perfect Professionals, LLC

Library of Congress Cataloging-in-Publication Data

Names: Allen, Judy.
Title: Ghostly graveyards / by Judy Allen ; consultant, Paul F. Johnston,
    PhD, historian, Washington, D.C.
Description: New York : Bearport Pub., 2016. I Series: Scary places I
    Includes bibliographical references and index.
Identifiers: LCCN 2015037683 I ISBN 9781943553082 (library binding) I ISBN
    1943553084 (library binding)
Subjects: LCSH: Haunted cemeteries—Juvenile literature.
Classification: LCC BF1474.3 .A45 2016 I DDC 133.1/22—dc23
LC record available at http://lccn.loc.gov/2015037683

For more information, write to Bearport Publishing Company, Inc., 45 West 21st Street, Suite 3B, New York, New York 10010. Printed in the United States of America.

10 9 8 7 6 5 4 3 2 1

Contents

By day, **graveyards** often look like peaceful parks filled with rolling lawns and tall trees. When night falls, though, things change. Moonlight casts an **eerie** glow on the **headstones**. Trees form creepy shapes and shadows. You might hear a distant cry echoing in the dark and feel a chill along your spine. Suddenly, out of the corner of your eye, you may notice a dark shadow creeping toward you, closer and closer. When you turn around to get a better look, it has disappeared, leaving you alone among the cold, gray stones.

In the 11 ghostly graveyards in this book, you will discover a blood-filled tree that's growing out of a grave, a mysterious lady in white who floats among headstones, a **poltergeist** that viciously attacks people, a vanishing house, a **funeral** party formed entirely of **phantoms**, and many other terrifying hauntings. So the next time you visit a graveyard, watch out! You never know what ghostly presence might be lurking.

The Vampire's Tree

El Panteón de Belén, Guadalajara, Mexico

In a small cemetery in Guadalajara, Mexico, there's a towering twisted tree. If you look closely, you'll see that the huge tree appears to be growing out of a grave. Whose grave is it, and how did the mysterious tree get there?

El Panteón de Belén, known as Santa Paula Cemetery, opened in 1848.

More than 150 years ago, the people of Guadalajara, Mexico, began finding small dead animals scattered around the city. There was something very strange about the tiny **corpses**—they had been drained of their blood. Soon after, babies were found dead in their cribs. They, too, had been emptied of blood. People began to suspect that a vampire was feasting on their loved ones.

The people of Guadalajara feared for their lives. So a group of brave townspeople decided to track down the vampire and put an end to the killings. One night, after a new corpse had been discovered, the group saw a strange man with pale skin creeping in the shadows. They were certain they had found their vampire killer. The townspeople grabbed the man and plunged a **wooden stake** through his heart. The next day, the people buried his body in a grave in El Panteón de Belén Cemetery, with the stake still in place. They placed the body under heavy concrete to prevent it from rising from the dead and escaping.

Months later, the stake began to grow into a tree. Over the years, the tree split the concrete and grew to be enormous. Some people believe that if you break a branch off the tree, the vampire's blood will ooze out of it.

The vampire's tree

Today, a tall fence surrounds the tree to protect it. People say that if the tree is cut down or dies, the vampire will rise from the grave and kill again.

7

Ghost Town Graves

La Noria Cemetery, La Noria, Chile

La Noria is a small abandoned town in Chile located in the driest place on Earth—the Atacama Desert. In the late 1800s, the people who lived in the town worked in mines harvesting a kind of salt called **saltpeter**. When the mines closed, the people moved away. Today, little is left of the town except broken machinery, **derelict** houses, graves—and the occasional ghost.

La Noria Cemetery

Life for La Noria's miners was very difficult. In addition to their backbreaking work, the owners of the mine treated their workers very badly. As a result, many of the miners died young. They were then buried in shallow graves in the sandy soil of La Noria Cemetery. Over time, the hot desert wind has blown the sand from some of the graves, revealing whole skeletons and grinning skulls. Shreds of clothing still hang off the dry, jagged bones.

Some people claim that the spirits of the dead miners remain in the town. It is said that ghostly figures wander through the empty streets at night, and **disembodied** voices whisper and weep in the cemetery at dusk. Residents of the nearby town of Iquique warn visitors not to go to La Noria. They believe that the ghostly miners are looking for **eternal** companions.

Saltpeter was once so valuable, it was called white gold. In the past, it was made into gunpowder and fertilizer. Then scientists discovered how to manufacture it. As a result, most of the saltpeter mines in Chile closed.

saltpeter

An open grave at
La Noria Cemetery

Beware of the Poltergeist!

Greyfriars Kirkyard, Edinburgh, Scotland

Greyfriars Kirkyard is an old church graveyard that dates back to the 1500s. It was built on the site of an ancient **monastery** that was later used as a prison. Many of the gravestones in Greyfriars Kirkyard have skulls and other images of death carved into them, but something far more disturbing lingers in the old cemetery.

Greyfriars Kirkyard

In the 1600s, King Charles II of England tried to force the Scottish people to change their religion. Many Scots refused. Disobeying the king, however, was against the law and resulted in arrest. A harsh judge named George Mackenzie forced the Scots who were arrested to await trial in a prison built in the churchyard. Many of the prisoners died from the cold and **starvation** and were buried where they fell. Other prisoners were sentenced to death by the judge. When Mackenzie finally died, he was buried in a tomb in Greyfriars Kirkyard. It's hardly surprising that a vicious poltergeist now haunts this place.

One night in 1998, a man broke into Mackenzie's tomb and damaged his coffin. According to legend, the man awoke a spirit that should have been left alone. The poltergeist has pinched, bruised, and terrified many visitors. It can strike anywhere in the cemetery—but is especially active near Mackenzie's tomb and inside the old prison. Guides who give tours of the graveyard always warn people to enter Greyfriars Kirkyard at their own risk.

A statue of
Greyfriars Bobby

The tomb of
George Mackenzie

In the 1800s, a loyal dog named Greyfriars Bobby spent 14 years guarding his dead owner's grave at Greyfriars Kirkyard. Local people fed the terrier until he died and was buried near his master.

The House that Haunts

Bachelor's Grove Cemetery, Chicago, Illinois

Near a thick forest in a suburb of Chicago is Bachelor's Grove Cemetery. It's not just any cemetery. In fact, it's one of the most haunted places in the United States. There have been more than 100 documented reports of ghostly sightings there, including a phantom farmhouse that disappears and then reappears.

Bachelor's Grove Cemetery

You've probably heard of haunted houses, but have you heard of a house that haunts? According to witnesses, there's a white two-story farmhouse nestled among some trees near the cemetery. A lamp burns brightly in the upstairs window. When visitors walk toward the building, however, it shrinks before their very eyes! Then it disappears into thin air. According to legend, if you try to enter the house, you will be trapped inside . . . forever.

In addition to the disappearing house, drivers on a road near the cemetery have spotted **orbs** of blue light dancing among the trees. They have also seen a fast-moving red light that looks like a streak of blood in the sky. In the 1970s, forest rangers on night watch noticed something even more peculiar at a nearby pond. They saw the ghostly image of an old man driving a horse and plow out of the pond. The rangers had no idea that in the 1870s, an old man lived nearby and used a horse to plow his fields. One day, something scared his horse, and it galloped straight into the pond. The man was caught in the reins. He couldn't free himself or the horse from the heavy plow and they both drowned.

In 1991, a group of ghost hunters explored the cemetery after dark. They saw nothing unusual but took **infrared** photographs. One photo revealed a partly see-through woman sitting on a gravestone.

13

The Gliding Nun

Barnes Old Cemetery, London, England

Barnes Old Cemetery is half-hidden among trees and tangled ivy in a London park. In the late 1870s, the victim of a violent murder was buried in the cemetery. Ever since that time, there have been reports of a pale nun-like figure gliding back and forth among the headstones. Who is she, and what is she looking for?

A headless statue at Barnes Old Cemetery

In 1879, something horrifying washed up on the shores of the River Thames, near Barnes Old Cemetery. It was a box containing the bones of a woman. However, one important piece of the skeleton was missing—the skull. Because the woman was never identified, her bones were buried in an unmarked grave. That's when the gliding white figure of a nun was first seen at Barnes Old Cemetery.

Later, it was discovered that the skeleton was that of 55-year-old Julia Martha Thomas, who had lived near the River Thames in the late 1800s. In 1879, Mrs. Thomas hired a maid named Kate Webster, who had a criminal past and a bad temper. After an argument with Mrs. Thomas, Kate admitted that she became so angry that she pushed Mrs. Thomas down the stairs and killed her. Kate got rid of the body by cutting it up, removing the head, and then boiling the flesh off the bones. Finally, she put the bones inside a box and tossed it into the river.

Is the ghostly figure at the Barnes Old Cemetery not a nun after all? Is it the spirit of Mrs. Thomas, hovering over her grave?

In 2010, Mrs. Thomas's skull was discovered buried in a garden near her old house.

Kate Webster, the murderer

15

The Haunted Road and the Hanged Man

El Campo Santo Cemetery, San Diego, California

El Campo Santo, which means "The Holy Field" in Spanish, is a cemetery in San Diego that was built in the mid-1800s on land that once belonged to Native Americans. The first people buried in the cemetery were **pioneer** families. In 1889, a street was built through it, on top of at least 20 graves. Many people believe this awoke and angered the spirits of the dead.

Graves at El Campo Santo Cemetery

People who live near El Campo Santo Cemetery have noticed some very strange things. Car alarms blare for no obvious reason, and cars that are parked near the cemetery often break down. Some people claim to feel an icy chill in the air, even on the hottest days.

What's even stranger is the tall, shadowy figure who lingers around one of the graves. The ghost is thought to be Yankee Jim Robinson. In 1852, Yankee Jim was convicted of stealing a boat. He was sentenced to death and hanged from a **gallows**. "He swung back and forth like a **pendulum** until he strangled to death," according to a local newspaper reporter. Yankee Jim's body was then buried in the cemetery. Just before his **execution**, Yankee Jim cried out that he was innocent. Is this why his spirit is not at peace?

REMEMBERING THE MORE THAN 20 MEN, WOMEN AND CHILDREN WHO LIE BURIED BENEATH SAN DIEGO AVE. ONLY ASSEMBLYMAN EDWARD L. GREENE WAS EXHUMED AND PLACED WITHIN THE NEW BOUNDARY OF EL CAMPO SANTO CEMETERY.

THESE GRAVES WERE DISCOVERED WITH THE USE OF GROUND PENETRATING RADAR IN 1993.

REST IN PEACE

THIS PLAQUE WAS PLACED BY THE HISTORICAL SHRINE FOUNDATION WITH FUNDS FROM THE SAN DIEGO COMMUNITY DEVELOPMENT BLOCK GRANT IN 1994.

San Diego Avenue

Visitors to the cemetery sometimes see a Native American dressed in traditional clothes. Many people think he is the cemetery watchman. Perhaps he is. Approach him to ask a question, though, and he will simply disappear.

The street that now covers some of the graves at El Campo Santo Cemetery is called San Diego Avenue.

Phantom Funerals

Greenwood Cemetery, Decatur, Illinois

According to legend, Greenwood Cemetery was originally a Native American burial ground. Traditionally, Native Americans do not mark their graves, so it is hard to tell where the dead are buried. In the mid 1800s, the people of Decatur created a cemetery of their own and may have accidentally disturbed the ancient graves.

Greenwood Cemetery

One of the most haunted places in Greenwood Cemetery was a huge **mausoleum**. Visitors passing by it would hear screaming and banging coming from inside the large, locked tomb. By the 1950s, the mausoleum had been badly damaged by weather and **vandals** and was torn down. Bodies inside the mausoleum not claimed by relatives were dumped in a mass grave. Today, as visitors walk over the site where the mausoleum once stood, they often notice the air grows dramatically colder.

Something even spookier happens at the cemetery. Sometimes gardeners working in the cemetery or people visiting a grave have claimed to see a funeral **procession**—made up entirely of ghosts! If the procession appears, gardeners respectfully move out of the way. Visitors to the cemetery do the same. Then the phantom funeral party simply vanishes.

Some people believe that ghosts and spirits absorb heat from the air, which can make the temperature drop. So a sudden unexpected chill may mean a ghost is near.

Voices from the Mausoleum

Toowong Cemetery, Brisbane, Australia

Sometimes a person with a troubled past is unable to rest after he or she dies. That person may decide to haunt and torment the living. Could this be what happened to a butcher named Patrick Mayne who lived in Australia in the 1800s?

Toowong Cemetery

In 1848, police found the bloody remains of Robert Cox, a woodcutter. Robert had been murdered and then butchered into small pieces. Part of his body was dumped in the Brisbane River. His severed head was found in a nearby shed. According to police, Robert had just been paid for months of work, yet the large amount of money he was carrying was missing.

Patrick Mayne, a butcher with a violent temper, was suspected of the crime. He and Robert had recently been spotted together at a pub, and Patrick needed money to open a new butcher shop. It's believed that Patrick framed another man for the murder. That man was later found guilty and hanged.

There is a rumor that Patrick Mayne confessed to the killing before he died. Yet no one knows for sure.

When Patrick died, he was buried in a large, white mausoleum in Toowong Cemetery. Whether or not Patrick was guilty, the mausoleum is a frightening place. The air around it is often unexpectedly chilly. Visitors have claimed to hear thumps, angry voices, and crashes from deep inside the mausoleum. Could the sounds be coming from Patrick's restless spirit?

The mausoleum of the Mayne family

Patrick Mayne is believed to have been mentally ill. His five children never married or had children. Perhaps they feared passing down their father's "madness."

The Woman in White

Union Cemetery, Easton, Connecticut

The Union Cemetery in Easton dates back to the 1700s and lies where three major roads meet. It is said to be the most haunted location in Connecticut. Phantom voices and mysterious glowing orbs have been reported in or near the cemetery. Unexplained streaks and blurs of light have appeared on photographs taken by visitors. The ghostly sightings are not only reported from within the cemetery but spill out onto the roadways. People often report seeing a phantom woman in white leaping in front of their cars.

Union Cemetery

Visitors say that Union Cemetery is haunted by a mysterious woman with long dark hair wearing a white nightgown. She is The Woman in White, often called The White Lady, and has been spotted floating among the gravestones. No one knows who she was when she was alive. Some think she was murdered and her body was dumped in the cemetery. Others believe she is the spirit of a woman who murdered her husband and then killed herself. A third story says she died giving birth and is looking for her baby. Whoever she is, she has frightened many cemetery visitors, as well as people who are driving nearby. Sometimes, she appears suddenly, right in front of a moving car. Horrified drivers slam on their brakes and leap out of the car to check for a body. Yet the woman has vanished and all they find is an empty road.

Is this a spirit rising from a grave?

People are not allowed inside Union Cemetery after sundown. However, at night, ghost hunters sometimes take photographs through the fence that surrounds the graves. Some photos have shown what is thought to be spirit energy rising from the tombs.

23

A Ghostly Keeper

La Recoleta Cemetery, Buenos Aires, Argentina

La Recoleta has wide, tree-lined streets and thousands of small, beautiful buildings and sculptures. It covers 14 acres (5.7 hectares). The cemetery looks just like a small city, yet all the residents are dead.

La Recoleta Cemetery

In the early 1900s, David Allano, an Italian **immigrant**, was a caretaker at La Recoleta. He loved the cemetery and wanted it to be his final resting place. Throughout his life, he saved money to build an elaborate tomb. He even paid an Italian sculptor to create an image of himself in marble, with his broom, watering can, and keys. Legend says that when the tomb was finished, David took his own life. He was put to rest in his beloved cemetery. Today, many workers have claimed to hear an unusual sound when dawn breaks in La Recoleta. It's the rattling of the ghostly caretaker's keys.

Another chilling story tells of a young man who met a pretty girl near the cemetery. He took her out for the evening. On the way home, she felt cold, so he lent her his coat. The next day, the young man went to the girl's house to collect his coat. He was alarmed to find out from the girl's mother that the girl had died years earlier and was buried at La Recoleta Cemetery. The shocked boy went to the girl's mausoleum and found his coat lying just outside her tomb. The ghost is said to be Luz Maria Garcia Velloso, who died in 1925.

The tomb of David Allano, the ghostly caretaker of the cemetery

There are many important and famous people buried at La Recoleta, including past presidents of Argentina.

The Touch of a Cold Hand

The Burying Point Cemetery, Salem, Massachusetts

Imagine if someone accused you of being a witch. Then imagine being questioned by a cruel judge and sentenced to death—even though you had done nothing wrong. That's exactly what happened to many people in Salem, Massachusetts, in the late 1600s.

In 1692, three girls living in Salem became very ill. They screamed strange words and then collapsed. The doctor who treated them suspected **witchcraft**. The young girls were forced to admit that they had been **bewitched** and to identify

The Burying Point Cemetery

the witches who had put a spell on them. Confused and ill, the young girls named many local people, who were then tortured and put on trial. More than 200 people met this same fate. In all, 20 people were eventually hanged for witchcraft.

One innocent man, 81-year-old Giles Corey, was also accused of practicing witchcraft, but he refused to talk. As a result, he was forced to lie on the ground while heavy stones were placed on him. After three days he was crushed to death by the weight of the stones. It is said that he cursed the whole town before he died.

It is thought that Giles Corey's curse still hangs over Salem. Cemetery visitors have seen ghostly presences and have been overcome with feelings of grief and fear. The most terrifying of the reports are those that tell of the sudden touch of an invisible, icy hand. Could it be the angry spirit of Giles Corey?

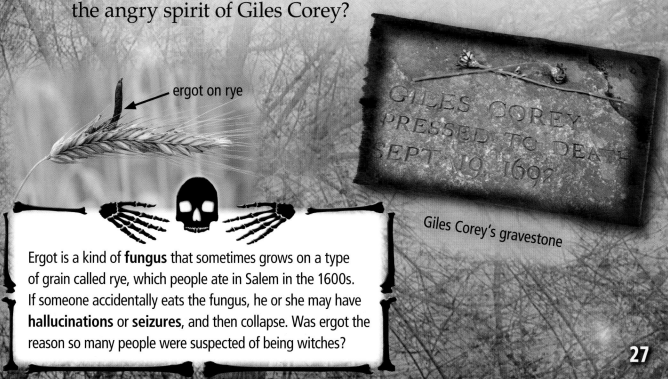

ergot on rye

Giles Corey's gravestone

Ergot is a kind of **fungus** that sometimes grows on a type of grain called rye, which people ate in Salem in the 1600s. If someone accidentally eats the fungus, he or she may have **hallucinations** or **seizures**, and then collapse. Was ergot the reason so many people were suspected of being witches?

Ghostly Graveyards

Greenwood Cemetery
Decatur, Illinois

The site of ghostly funerals

Bachelor's Grove Cemetery
Chicago, Illinois

Site of a vanishing farmhouse and a phantom farmer

Arctic Ocean

El Campo Santo Cemetery
San Diego, California

A cemetery covered by a road and haunted by a hanged man

NORTH AMERICA

The Burying Point Cemetery
Salem, Massachusetts

A place where angry spirits reach out to visitors

Union Cemetery
Easton, Connecticut

Haunted by a ghostly woman in white

Pacific Ocean

Atlantic Ocean

El Panteón de Belén
Guadalajara, Mexico

Site of a vampire's grave and a blood-filled tree

SOUTH AMERICA

La Recoleta Cemetery
Buenos Aires, Argentina

Home to thousands of mausoleums . . . and ghosts

La Noria Cemetery
La Noria, Chile

Where the ghosts of dead miners walk among shallow graves

Around the World

Greyfriars Kirkyard
Edinburgh, Scotland

Home of a violent poltergeist

EUROPE

ASIA

Barnes Old Cemetery
London, England

A place where a famous murder victim is buried and a gliding spirit has been seen

AFRICA

Toowong Cemetery
Brisbane, Australia

The final resting place of an angry butcher— and possible murderer

Indian Ocean

AUSTRALIA

Southern Ocean

ANTARCTICA

Glossary

bewitched (bi-WICHT) affected by witchcraft; placed under a spell

corpses (KORPS-iz) dead bodies

derelict (DER-*uh*-likt) left or deserted; abandoned

disembodied (dis-em-BOD-eed) separated from or existing without a body

eerie (EER-ee) mysterious, strange

eternal (i-TUR-nuhl) an endless time period

execution (eks-uh-KYOO-shuhn) putting a person to death

funeral (FYOO-nuh-ruhl) a ceremony that is held after a person dies

fungus (FUHN-guhss) a plantlike organism that can't make its own food, such as a mushroom

gallows (GAL-ohz) a wooden structure from which people are hanged

graveyards (GRAYV-yardz) places where dead people or animals are buried

hallucinations (huh-*loo*-suh-NAY-shuhnz) seeing or hearing things that aren't there

headstones (HED-stonz) slabs of stone set up at the tops of graves

immigrant (IM-uh-gruhnt) a person who comes from one country to live in a new one

infrared (in-fruh-RED) a form of energy that is similar to light but can't be seen by the human eye

mausoleum (maw-*suh*-LEE-uhm) a burial place, usually in the form of a small building

monastery (MON-uh-stair-ee) a place where people who have devoted their lives to their faith work and live

orbs (AWRBS) glowing spheres

pendulum (PEN-juh-luhm) a weight that moves from side to side

phantoms (FAN-tuhms) ghosts or spirits

pioneer (*pye*-uh-NEER) a person who goes to live in a place that is not yet settled

poltergeist (POHL-tur-gyest) a disruptive ghost that makes loud noises and moves objects

procession (pruh-SESH-uhn) a group of people walking along a route as part of a religious service

saltpeter (sawlt-PEE-tur) a kind of salt that occurs naturally

seizures (SEE-zhurz) sudden fits that can cause a person to shake and even lose consciousness

starvation (star-VAY-shuhn) to suffer or die from hunger

vandals (VAN-duhls) people who needlessly damage or destroy other people's property

witchcraft (WICH-kraft) the actions or magical powers of a witch

wooden stake (WUD-uhn STAYK) a piece of wood with a sharp point at the end

Bibliography

Austin, Joanne. *Weird Hauntings: True Tales of Ghostly Places.* New York: Sterling (2006).

Hauck, Dennis William. *Haunted Places: The National Directory: Ghostly Abodes, Sacred Sites, UFO Landings, and Other Supernatural Locations.* New York: Penguin (2002).

Henderson, Jan-Andrew. *The Ghost That Haunted Itself: The Gruesome Ghoul of Edinburgh's Greyfriars Graveyard.* Edinburgh: Mainstream Publishing (2001).

Read More

Hamilton, John. *Haunted Places (The World of Horror).* Edina, MN: ABDO (2007).

Stern, Steven L. *Cursed Grounds (Scary Places).* New York: Bearport (2011).

Williams, Dinah. *Spooky Cemeteries (Scary Places).* New York: Bearport (2008).

Learn More Online

To learn more about ghostly graveyards, visit
www.bearportpublishing.com/ScaryPlaces

Index

About the Author

Judy Allen is the award-winning author of more than 60 books for children, both fiction and nonfiction. She lives near Barnes Old Cemetery.